The LIGHT in the LIVING ROOM

Dad's Messages
from the
Other Side

....

**As told through JOHN McKIBBIN
to GATES McKIBBIN**

LIFELINES LIBRARY

In light and love,

Gates McKibbin

For information, contact:

Field Flowers, Inc.
641 Healdsburg Avenue
Healdsburg, CA 95448
707 433 9771
www.fieldflowers.com
www.lifelineslibrary.com

Cover and text design by Kajun Design

Front cover detail from "Judith II (Salomé)"
by Gustav Klimt (Cameraphoto/Art Resource)

Author's photo by Christina Schmidhofer

ISBN 1-929799-00-4

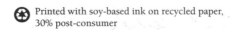

To my dear father, John Clark McKibbin,
who radiates the essence of eternal love—
and reaffirms eternal life

Also by Gates McKibbin:

LoveLines: Notes on Loving and Being Loved

A Course in Courage: Disarming the Darkness with Strength of Heart

A Handbook on Hope: Fusing Optimism and Action

The Life of the Soul: The Path of Spirit in Your Lifetimes

Available Wisdom: Insights from Beyond the Third Dimension

What began three years ago as a series of journal entries is now coming into the world as a series of books. All along the way people with the perspective and expertise I needed crossed my path at exactly the right time. Each person has contributed soul and substance to the project. I am abundantly grateful to:

♦ **Ned Engle**, who saw what my writings could become long before I did and then adroitly guided me there.

♦ **Barbra Dillenger, Michael Makay, Benjo Masilungan** and **Anthony Corso**, whose comments on each new manuscript reassured me of the accuracy and usefulness of the material.

♦ **Judith Appelbaum** and **Florence Janovic** at Sensible Solutions, whose savvy counsel about the publishing industry kept me confident and on course.

♦ **Carol Fall**, who offered discerning marketing advice and was the creative force behind the book titles.

♦ **Erin Blackwell** and **Cynthia Rubin**, whose editorial finesse honored and strengthened the messages.

♦ **Laurie Smith** and **Pat Koren** at Kajun Design, who transformed each book into a jewel within and without.

CONTENTS

GLOSSARY

Creation consists of multiple dimensions of reality. Each dimension is characterized by its vibratory or magnetic quality. The higher the frequency at which the dimension vibrates, the more at one it is with God. The **higher realms** are the dimensions of spiritual reality beyond the material world, where distinctions based on time and space do not exist.

Karma is composed of imprints on your soul created by your choices (thoughts, words and actions). Choices that embrace spirit heal, balance, complete and remove karmic imprints from your current and prior lifetimes that distance your soul from God. Choices that deny or avoid spirit add new imprints that must be healed, balanced, completed and removed later.

Your **lesson** is the larger karmic pattern or theme you are addressing during this lifetime.

Your **mission** is the major contribution you are making in this lifetime to enable the evolution of collective consciousness toward oneness with God.

Your **soul** is the vessel for your spirit. It carries an

infinite variety of karmic imprints that record the experiences your spirit has had, in and out of embodiment. Your soul is all love and light. It represents your limitless potential to embrace spirit to the fullest capacity.

Spirit guides are spiritual entities who have committed to helping you follow the path of love and contribute to the spiritual evolution of all creation. They whisper in your ear telepathically. They send you insights and intuitive flashes. They reaffirm your deepest inner knowing that there is a benevolent higher power inherent in all things.

The **third dimension** is the material reality on planet earth. It consists of dense physical matter that vibrates slowly. The third dimension is characterized by segmented linear time (past, present and future) and compartmentalized space (measurements, boundaries and separation).

The **veil** is a magnetic field surrounding planet earth that separates the vibratory capacity of the third dimension from that of the higher realms. It forms a barrier between your earthly awareness and your higher consciousness. The veil creates the illusion that material reality—and your survival in it—is your reason for being.

The term **we** that is used throughout this book refers to John McKibbin, the spirit who was Gates' father in this lifetime, and the other spiritual entities collaborating with him on the messages he sent down to her.

WISDOM to
LIGHT the WAY

In 1978 at age sixty-three my father, John McKibbin, died. For many people that would signal a complete departure of a loved one from their lives. But with Dad that has been far from the case. He began making his presence known to me almost immediately after his death, and he has continued to be a guiding light in my life ever since.

Dad may have left his physical body, but he can exert energy on the earth plane that is strong enough to turn on the floor lamp in my living room. When I return home from a long trip, invariably as I open the door the light is glowing to welcome me home. The lamp has a three-way mechanism in it, and the brightness increases the happier he seems to be that I made it back safe and sound. Normally the light is on low, but recently after a whitewater rafting trip when I had been tossed into the roiling rapids and rescued without a glitch, it was as bright as a floodlight.

Dad also turns on the light to attract my attention when he has something to tell me and I am too preoccupied to be aware of his presence. When the light comes on I stop whatever I am doing (including sleeping), lean against the arched entryway into the living room next to the lamp and ask out loud, "What do I need to know?"

Often he signals to me to grab pen and paper and begin writing what he has to tell me.

I never know what his messages will be. He may address an issue or question I am struggling with at the moment, or inform me that he has another book for me to bring down. Sometimes he simply wants to acknowledge the progress I've made.

This has been going on since the summer of 1996. Writing down these messages that he sends to me telepathically has become as natural as having a conversation with a friend. It is effortless. His presence is so integrated into my life, it is as if we are living under the same roof. In many ways, I suppose, we are.

This book contains the first written messages that Dad sent through me. They began arriving at a time in my life when I had hit the wall. Illness and burnout had forced me to extricate myself from the corporate fast lane. Reluctantly, I was confronting professional indecision and financial instability, and agonizing over how to regain my health, redefine my career and get my life back on track.

Dad helped me face those fears with straight talk and unconditional love.

There is nothing unusual about a parent's coming to the side of a son or daughter who is going through a tough time. It happens every day. My mother, spunky and sanguine at 82, has helped me through more scrapes than I can count. The difference is that Dad lives in the spiri-

6

tual realms—not in the material world as she does.

This sounds preposterous, I know. Here I am, a businesswoman with three decades of hard-won credibility under my belt, declaring that my dead father turns on the light in my living room and talks to me telepathically. Why would I ever want to go public with such declarations? Furthermore, who in her right mind would choose to endure the skeptics' inevitable charge of being simply another con artist selling the latest form of snake oil just in time for the millennium? Wouldn't it be better to stay in the spiritual closet?

I'll admit, I was tempted to do that. For quite a while only my closest friends and family knew of these goings-on. But one book led to another, then another. Almost before I knew it, I had completed six volumes. Somewhere along the way I realized that to refuse to share Dad's messages with others because of my own insecurities proved just one thing: that I hadn't heard a word he had said to me. So I established a publishing company to design and produce the books, created a joint venture to develop other products highlighting Dad's messages, and determined to spread the word as widely as possible.

Quite frankly, the other reason I decided to go public with my story is that after two decades of my father's integral presence in my life after his death, it seemed foolish to let a more pervasive notion of life (or lack thereof) after death limit my own. I know what I have experienced, and it is Dad's spiritual nearness to me. He has been with me and around me ever since his death.

Dad's visits began about a month after he died. I awoke one night startled by a weight pushing down on

7

my toes. I thought that someone had broken into my apartment and come into my bedroom. But the minute I opened my eyes, the pressure vanished. A week later it happened again. This time I was less frightened. As I lay still with my eyes closed trying to figure out what was going on, I had a strong sense of Dad's presence. In fact, I was sure it was Dad. He returned often. Along the way I became more comfortable with the idea that he could still be with me, albeit in a different form.

I didn't tell anyone about these encounters. It all seemed too weird. And what if I was just imagining that a dead person could come back in spirit?

My father had been a rock-steady, humble, unexcitable man. It seemed totally out of character for him to do anything as unforeseen and dramatic as returning to the physical plane after his death. Little did I know that his visits would lead to something even more unforeseen and dramatic—messages channeled through him to me from the other side of the veil.

Dad was a civil engineer by trade. He spent a good part of his career buying right-of-way for the construction of the state and interstate highways that link the cities and towns in Illinois. Usually his work required him to purchase the land from families that had been farming it for generations. They weren't always happy to be letting it go so that more cars could get more places faster. But Dad would get to know them first, listen to all the reasons why it was a hardship for them to sell a strip of their land to the state, offer them a fair price and explain to them why it was a fair price. His cases rarely ended up in court.

As a result of his work, Dad got to know a lot of people throughout central Illinois. We couldn't go anywhere without his telling us all about Mrs. Carlson, who was up in years but still had one of the best vegetable gardens around, or the Finney family, which had been farming the same 750 acres since 1823. One summer in particular he would occasionally stop by the house spur-of-the-moment, load us all up in the car, and drive us to Fishook, which had an old general store he had discovered. He would take care of business with one of the farmers nearby, and we would explore the musty old place's nooks and crannies. You can't say "Fishook" to anyone in the family without bringing back memories of country-fresh eggs and the biggest five-cent Baby Ruths we'd ever seen.

My siblings and I grew up hearing Dad say, "If you can't do something right, don't do it at all." He lived by that standard and expected everyone else in the family to do so as well.

Nothing escaped him. If one of us was even a little bit off, whether it involved hammering a nail straight or throwing a runner out at third base, he saw it and told us in detail how to do it better the next time. It was tough trying to be as adept as adults when our ages weren't yet in the double digits, but we often were. We wanted to please Dad; we sensed that the reason he placed the bar so high for us was that he just knew we could clear it.

For me, the hurdles to clear were supposed to have included finishing college, getting married, working a few years, having children, joining the PTA—and not straying too far from the Midwest. I had gotten married, all right, and returned to my hometown after college. But then I discovered that I loved working, so I put off having a family. Based on my track record at work, I was awarded a fellowship for a doctoral program that was too good an opportunity to turn down. That led to a divorce, which opened the door for me to move to the West Coast.

I spent the next 18 years as a single woman pursuing a career and a spiritual path with equal zeal. I consulted with corporate clients about strategy, organization and leadership. I wrote business articles, conducted seminars and built an extensive professional network. I also practiced Zen meditation and went to an ashram in India. I learned how to read astrological charts and tarot cards and the *I Ching*. I explored past lives to discover their connection with this one. I read metaphysical literature and poked around in all kinds of alternative ways to make sense of what was happening.

I was also paying the mortgage and recycling the junk mail and maintaining close relationships with family and friends.

When something stymied me after Dad's death, he would appear out of the blue. He would flood into my consciousness with a love that was so overwhelming, all I could do was cry. It never occurred to me that Dad might actually be leading me around the obstacle I was facing, though soon afterward I would often find my way past it.

Then in 1996 his visits became more frequent and profound. It was a traumatic time for me. I had developed a tenacious case of pneumonia. Run-down and stressed out, I knew I had a choice: take some drastic measures to lead a healthier life, or do nothing and let my body take even more drastic measures. I chose the former option. I quit my job.

My physical condition was precarious, and I had walked away from my financial security. I decided to begin writing in a journal every day to address the unsettling changes I had introduced into my life. The very first morning while I was journaling, I felt Dad arrive. He told me telepathically that he had important messages for me that I should write in my journal. Not at all confident that I could understand what he had to say, I turned to a new sheet anyway and wrote "Dad Page" at the top. Somehow I was able to hear him, and I let my hand write his words. The first entry in this book is what he told me that day.

Each morning when I began writing, I both anticipated and was apprehensive about whether Dad would appear. I wondered, what if I never hear from him again? What if this isn't Dad at all, but my desire to be in touch with his spirit? What if he is here but I am not aware of it?

To assuage my uncertainty, Dad would flood me with a tidal wave of love every time he had a message for me. When I became accustomed to the process of accessing his words, he asked me to continue without such reassurance. It took a great deal of his energy to provide it in such a forceful way.

Dad's guidance became invaluable in helping me navigate the unknowns into which I had thrust myself. His messages were a mixture of support and encouragement, wisdom and candor. He named my fears and helped me transcend them. He revealed the larger context for my life, framing time and space in a totally different way. He nudged and cajoled, celebrated and comforted.

In time Dad told me that his messages weren't meant for me alone—that they needed to be made available to others as well. He suggested that I type my handwritten journal entries from him into the computer, then review the material.

Doing that helped me realize the wealth of insight in his messages. From there I deleted the personal context and focused on the universal themes embedded in each message. *The Light in the Living Room* is what emerged.

This is wisdom handed down from father to daughter, and now from daughter to other fathers and daughters, mothers and sons, friends and family. May it light the way for you as it has for me.

FATHER and DAUGHTER

I love you, dearest Gates. You cannot fathom the depths of my love for you because you are not wholly in spirit as I am. Yet you know of my love and my presence in your life.

I have been coming to you often since my death. At first I had difficulty making the adjustment between the two planes. When I got more adept at it, you became more aware of my visits.

Please know that my being with you is not a burden for me at all. It brings me great joy, especially when I can see that in some way I have helped you. Only recently have you begun to understand the complexity of your being. I will help you go even further along the spiritual dimension of your existence.

You have come a long way already. I want you to begin bringing down the information I have for you. You can either write what I have to tell you in longhand or sit at your computer. There is no difference in your ability to receive the information. For now, use your journal. It is a more comfortable and familiar medium.

The process we are engaged in now is similar to what we did when you were a young girl learning to ride a two-wheeler. When the training wheels were on the bicycle, you could ride alone. Then I took them off and ran beside you with my hand on the seat. When I knew you had control of the bicycle, I took my hand off the seat but still ran beside you to provide you with the sense of security and safety that you needed. Later I told you that you had kept your balance on your own.

We will follow the same method here.

You cannot fail. You will not fall.

I walk the path with you always.

CONVERSATION

You know how much I love you. You know how devoted I am to you. I am joyful that you have discovered this means for me to communicate with you.

What is occurring is like a conversation between two spirits who love each other very much. Without the love's going both ways you would not be able to receive what I have to say. Your heart would not fill to overwhelming.

But you do know me as a loving spiritual presence in your life. And I feel your love. It is a great blessing for me. There is no need ever to feel alone, for I am with you more often than I would be if I were still in embodiment. That is the irony of my having left my body when I did.

Love is a vibrational and spiritual dynamic. It does heal. It does renew. It does live in everyone, no matter how loveless they may seem on the surface.

The love crystal is present in every being in embodiment. God is incapable of producing anything that does not contain the love essence as its foundation element. Pure love is pure spirit. We are companions in spirit and love.

DARKNESS and LIGHT

We all derive from the same source. We are all one.

But this unity is not pure as is the God-source. Over time darkness was seeded throughout creation and like weeds growing in a garden, it has maintained a tenacious hold over the weaknesses of spirit.

Nowhere more clearly than on earth do we have more evidence of the epic struggle between darkness and light. In one form or another everyone who is in embodiment contends with this dynamic. That is the essence of being human. Without darkness there would be no opportunity for growth—no opportunity to rise above and beyond limitation.

It was absolutely necessary to include the forces of darkness in the plan.

How much of a risk was it for God to do that? It was a great risk and no risk at all. On the one hand, darkness can, does and has predominated. But only temporarily. On the other hand, light is more powerful—always, endlessly. Spirit eliminates the forces of darkness immediately when people allow it in.

Although spirit is present everywhere at all times, people must consciously welcome it into their reality in the moment. Otherwise, it has no influence. So the clash between light and darkness is really about each person's own individual journey. It is a journey of love confounded by opposite forces. Those challenges will never end.

Each person has the ability to bring in spirit, to incorporate love into everything he or she does. For within everyone is unlimited potential for the light to prevail.

INTEGRITY

The interplay of darkness and light is full of deception and intrigue. It is all about things not being as they appear to be. Darkness works by being something that it isn't. This often creates fear, uncertainty, guilt and other emotions that destroy confidence and fuel doubt.

The minute honesty enters into such a situation, darkness is threatened. Like the light as it dispels the darkness in a room, integrity expels the influence of darkness.

But it is much more complicated than that. Why? Although light is evident to anyone in a room—except those who are asleep or blind—the influence of truth in an environment of falsity is not as immediately apparent. People continue to behave as they did before the truth entered. They cannot recognize it. They do not see it. They cannot allow it in. They are like a blind person in a room with light. They are like someone sleeping through the midday sun with the shades drawn.

So with that in mind, you must think through your options at any given moment and select the course that is truthful and light-infused. What you do will vary from situation to situation.

Sometimes taking overt responsibility with your words and deeds is appropriate—if that is your truth at the time. Sometimes challenging another person—or even engaging in open conflict—is the best course. Sometimes saying nothing and honoring your own truth within by walking away is the only option. That is fitting when the tide of blackness is stronger than your ability to shift it, even with a massive infusion of your capacity.

Deciding the best course of action—or nonaction—is not as difficult as you may think. Follow this simple process. Ask yourself:

- What is my truth in this situation?
- What is my intuition telling me to do?
- How much of an impact can I realistically have?
- What action can I take that intensifies the integrity of the situation without costing me more than it is worth?

MOON

You challenge the darkness with your light.

But like the light that glows from a full moon, yours has become more subtle even as it grows more powerful. You no longer need to radiate as the sun does, although it is in your nature to do so.

The light that emanates from you now is softer and more gentle, brighter and more certain. It lights the way for pilgrims through the darkness they face on their own journeys.

The path is always there, even when it seems totally obscured. The moon helps people find it and follow it. It doesn't lead them or pick them up when they stumble or create day in the middle of night. Rather, it is a source of gentle guidance, inner knowing, inspiration and hope.

It works quietly. It often isn't acknowledged for its contribution. People take it for granted. Yet in some ways it is the most beautiful body in the heavens. It is the feminine principle embodied for all.

CONFORM and TRANSFORM

Consider the distinction between *con*form and *trans*-form. The two prefixes represent a universe of difference.

Conformity requires changes toward a predetermined standard, which remains stable. Conformity is based on an evaluation that one state of being is preferable to another, and thus things would be "better" if shifts occurred in that direction.

Transformation, on the other hand, demands that everything be challenged and perhaps altered significantly without knowledge of the end point. Everyone involved must be willing to surrender to the infinite possibilities of forming something truly new and transcendental.

Transformation requires you to leap into the unknown.

Conformity requires you to leap into the known.

NO-THING

You are in a vortex of massive change. People are feeling it as too much to do, too much pressure, borderline burnout.

Remember to maintain a calm center in the middle of the chaos. Keep people at bay if you must. Manage your time with them. Preserve time alone. You are as stretched as everyone else. But you have solid grounding in spirit, so you can maintain a workable equilibrium.

Take care of yourself first and foremost. Others will want to lean on you more, and you must pay attention to how you are spending every moment of every day.

Find ways to replenish and nourish yourself. If you are always going, always working, you create no room to hear the silence.

Maintain the perspective that your work also includes non-work—meandering through your favorite neighborhoods, sipping a cup of tea, contemplating a beautiful sunrise.

What else must you do? Nothing. No-thing.

That is a huge challenge, to let go and do no-thing.

In doing no-thing you are trusting the process. You are affirming that there is an invisible path and a plan— that the best path is surrendering to the unknowable.

SAFETY

You crave solitude. Sometimes when you get home you resist opening your mail or listening to your phone messages. Do not berate yourself for needing this uninterrupted solitude. It is a gift you can give yourself.

Simply stated, you are giving yourself unconditional safety at home. That is neither selfish nor unhealthy.

RECEIVING

You are blessed beyond measure. Your cup overflows with love and kindness from your friends, family and spirits. Never believe that you are alone or without resources.

You have support—always. Call on it when you need it. We all love you.

You can receive unconditional love from others who want to give back to you. Accept their gifts—with no strings attached.

Learn to allow their blessings to flow into and through you.

LOVE and OPTIMISM

You love and are dearly loved.

You are also optimistic about your future.

Love and optimism are two guiding words for your future. They relate to how you should approach everything. They comprise your mantra for a while.

Love without optimism can become destructive, codependent. It can limit as much as it lifts. Optimism without love has no grounding and therefore rarely is a source of energy or effectiveness.

But the two together form the space for vision and hope, action and attainment.

Make that space within yourself. Hold it, for it is precious. Be clear about its value. It should not be compromised—ever.

Use these two words to evaluate the people and situations that come your way. If they fuel your optimism and are rooted in love, then move ahead with them. If they make you lose your optimism or cause you to doubt yourself unnecessarily, avoid them.

Nothing is worth the erosion of either love or optimism. For they are the essence of spirit. They lead to peace and joy. Choose that. It is time. You deserve it.

The world exists as a place for your marvelous unfolding and will support you in that.

WISDOM and COMPASSION

You are developing a deep sense of the interconnectedness of all things.

Your certainty of that is your sword. It is also your shield. You need both, for going out unprotected into the world is neither wise nor compassionate.

True compassion is rooted in strength, not weakness or vulnerability. It is one thing to breathe in another's pain and hold it in a place of love. It is something far different to accept it as one's own. Taking on another's problem is disempowering for the other and debilitating for yourself. That is neither wise nor compassionate.

You serve others best when you help them discover and reaffirm their own inner knowing (wisdom) and move through their pain (compassion).

Nonetheless, you must use caution. Do not try to save the world—especially all at once!

Be thoughtful in your commitments and careful with your attention. Others still sap your strength more than you might anticipate. Try to reserve as much time as possible to be alone—to rejuvenate.

Think of yourself first. Remain healthy and strong and balanced. Stay at home in the quiet as much as you want. Use your free time to energize and heal and reaffirm spirit.

MEDITATIONS

Consider your current circumstances in the context of the following:

- Light conquers darkness.
  Your light is never absent.
  Therefore, darkness can never overtake you.
- Forgiveness heals, even if it is one-sided.
  Forgiveness is rooted in strength, not submission.
- Take care not to fall into self-pity.
- Do not look for logic.
- Remember that nothing is linear.
- Send love—not its opposite.
- There is much to anticipate.
- There is much to be grateful for.

CITY LIFE

Your energy is greatly depleted in urban areas. Your crystalline aura picks up energy around you and not only reflects it, but amplifies it. That is not healthy for you in the long run. You must find ways to deal with city life more effectively.

Here are some suggestions:

- Take a bath or shower at the end of the workday to cleanse the toxins you have picked up inadvertently and stored in your body and energy field.
- Give yourself time each day—morning and evening —to balance and recharge. Do this with love for yourself.
- Eat lightly and drink plenty of fresh fruit and vegetable juices.
- Be patient. Trust that you have the information that you need to make the appropriate choices.
- Concentrate on your dreams—not your limitations. Your dreams can become a reality any time you want them to.
- Trust that all is unfolding as it should.

- Recognize that great trauma and great transformation usually go hand-in-hand. That is the human condition.
- Recognize also that it is also the human condition to be dearly loved.

LIMINALITY

You are experiencing the process of liminality—of being at the threshold between two phases of your existence.

This is a key time in your life, when you are between definitions of who you are personally, in relationship, spiritually, energetically and professionally. Realize that your career changes are only a small fraction of the totality of shifts that are occurring now within you.

Little is staying the same for you, except the very foundation of your being—the vision that you brought into this lifetime and have been enhancing since your birth.

The rest is falling away. New frames and structures, concepts and fluidities, vibrational and magnetic forces have not yet taken their places within you.

Relish this rare interlude rather than wishing it were over.

BEING LOVED

How much are you loved?

Imagine all the light you will see during every waking moment of your lifetime. Every minute outdoors during the day, every awareness of the sun shining when you're indoors, the stars—each one, the moon and its moonbeams, prisms shining through crystals, smiles and sparkling eyes, entities showering you with golden rays, fairies scattering pixie dust about. Compile all of that, and it is only a fraction of the love you receive every moment of every day.

BEING LOVE

When you are overwhelmed with love, the feeling of love is fourth-dimensional in its essence but felt physically in the third dimension. Your body has enormous capacity to feel and express love. And in the fourth dimension you *are* love.

Bridge the two at all times. As you continue in this embodiment, you must be love in the third dimension to the same extent that you are love in the fourth dimension—and eventually even higher dimensions.

You have enhanced your ability to embody and communicate love. Others can now receive it more openly, and thus it can flow through you more magnanimously.

To be love requires two prerequisites: the ability of others to receive that love and the ability of the giver to accept love from others.

It really is that simple and that difficult.

INITIATION

The book you found about female initiation rites in Pompeii has helped you understand that feminine strength is born of *both* masculine experience and awareness *and* feminine affirmation and integration. It is not synonymous with the virginal feminine, who is whole unto herself without experience of the masculine. Rather, it is about wisdom, which arises from death and rebirth— death of the unevolved feminine at the hands of masculine strength and rebirth into feminine power.

Recognize that this would not be possible without masculine capability and the overwhelming way in which it threatens the feminine. The dominance of the male is a gift cloaked as a challenge to the female and should be recognized and honored as such.

Male initiation rites emphasize both the need for self-reliance and the path to such, which is the inner or feminine path. So males have a different experience that involves themselves alone, going deep within. Those who survive it return not more powerful in terms of what they can do physically, but more in touch with the spirit that guides and protects them. Their access to that spirit derives from the feminine that breathes within them.

REWARDS

The last few years have been difficult. You have come through the trials with a renewed sense of spirit and self. You are about to reap the rewards.

Don't expect these rewards to look like a vacation under the palm trees. Instead, they will manifest as catalysts for your continued evolution. You will be pushed as far and as fast as you can go.

There is a great deal of work to be done…and plenty of love to keep it on track.

You will, of course, also have an occasional respite under the palms.

GUIDANCE

The issue in the relationship in question is whether you can guide each other to the harbor. That can be done only with purity of heart and innocence of intent.

Here are some thoughts to illuminate the way:

♦ Detach from the need to know the outcome.

♦ Love unconditionally.

♦ Refrain from pursuing any agenda, hidden or overt.

♦ Keep an open mind and an open heart.

♦ Anticipate the unexpected.

♦ Allow yourself to be guided.

♦ Know that you are loved in many ways that you do not recognize or understand.

♦ Appreciate the fact that you are on a dynamic path toward your karmic completion.

♦ Be kind to yourself. You are on course, even if it doesn't feel like it.

BLESSINGS

Recall your blessings.

Remember that you are God incarnate—that the source of love and light is with you and within you always.

Embrace each day with gratitude from dawn till dusk. Pray to be a vehicle of God's work and make yourself a vessel for God's words.

Treat yourself with the same respect you accord others. Be generous of heart and hand, but do not give so much that you are bereft of resources, be they inner or outer.

Follow your path. Walk nimbly and with a sure foot.

Keep your faith, for you are light and love, more and more so each day.

Go in peace.

CONTAINER

There is a difference between living for the future as it is defined by one human embodiment and living with the future of the soul as the end point. When the future is defined in the former way, then one is likely to live from the outside in. When the future is defined in the latter way, one lives from the inside out.

For years I, with and through others, have been teaching you about the other side of the veil. We have been expanding your sense of time and eliminating the limitations you had previously placed upon the notion of existence. You now cannot conceive of your existence as anything other than soul and spirit in the infinite.

Once this sense of being is well established, it is possible both to live in the moment and simultaneously to act and make choices with your soul's ultimate reality in mind (in this and other dimensions both now and in the future). You no longer have the luxury of doing one thing for the single purpose of serving your immediate survival only.

What limits you most when you are in embodiment

is the context in which you place your existence. If your frame of reference is that you are disconnected from all of life; if your frame of reference is that you have just one lifetime; if your frame of reference is that only the third dimension is available to you; if you believe only what you see, you create a constricted container for growth and renewal and enlightenment.

Expand your container from within. Reaffirm the infinite existence of your soul.

PURPOSE

You have come through one of the most challenging stages of your life. It took you to the edge both personally and professionally. This gave you an opportunity to gain strength of self and clarity of intent once you faced the situation and got through it.

You are on the other side of that now, and as a result your sense of purpose is broader and more relaxed.

This is good.

It is good because your life has been dominated by work-related purpose. Like many others in this culture—and on the planet as a whole—you have focused on making significant professional contributions. For decades you have invested extraordinary amounts of yourself in your work. Everything else was secondary.

That is no longer the case.

Consider the implications and rejoice.

TUG-of-WAR

You have been feeling disoriented lately. You have come face-to-face with the entrenched closed-mindedness that keeps the limitations of the third dimension intact. You have seen yourself through others' eyes and have wondered whether you have gone too far in your explorations—whether you have been duped into believing something manufactured out of ego and not metaphysical reality.

This is worthwhile—not so much because of the accuracy of others' perceptions and judgments but as a reminder that you are far afield of mainstream thinking. That is a reality you have lived with most of your life.

It is just more extreme now.

And those extremes reflect the fundamental polarities that are currently in a tug-of-war. Will higher consciousness prevail, with its larger sense of human possibilities? Or will resistance to that create an even thicker veil than what existed previously? There is always the risk, when polarities are so excessive, that a backlash will overpower the forces of enlightened progress.

So we move into a much more intense time. You will feel that you have lost your grounding, but that will not be the case at all. Rather, you are enhancing your understanding of the forces at work. This will help you recognize resistance more quickly when it comes toward you and then redirect its force toward transformation.

LIVING in
TWO WORLDS

You are being challenged to live in two worlds—to dwell beyond the material reality of the third dimension as well as in it. You believe that is easier said than done.

That is true and not so true.

You are able to access dimensions beyond the immediate physical plane each time you sit down with your journal or computer keyboard to write these messages. In the process you enter into a more valid reality than any other, because it encompasses the totality of you in the totality of creation.

Think of it: the totality of you in the totality of creation.

We require nothing less than that from you. And there is nothing more than that.

Nonetheless, living in the third dimension when you so long to transcend it is almost more than you can endure at times. You long to be home. You long to remember what you carried with you between lifetimes. You long to be free of confinement in your body as it travels through days and years in this mortal trajectory.

Living in the third dimension requires you to release your desire to control the dynamics and interplays of the immediate reality in which you find yourself. Your soul's journey is not a matter of control but of surrender. You know that. But impatience and insecurity lead you away from surrender.

Impatience and insecurity stimulate myriad questions you would like to have answered. Will you be on your way to Paris in a couple of weeks? How will your work evolve? Will you have the courage to stay the course you have embarked on spiritually?

These questions are both important and irrelevant. They are important because they occupy an inordinate amount of your time and attention. They are irrelevant because in the long run—meaning beyond lifetimes—they are mere ripples in the pond.

TIME

Time in other dimensions is infinitely expandable and simultaneously in the moment. In other dimensions one can see and link what you label in the third dimension as "past" and "future" while being absolutely within the current essence of the moment.

How is this possible?

Detachment. Detachment from the outcome of an action; detachment from fears and doubts; detachment from the need for material security; detachment from others as sources of affirmation and completion.

All of these forms of detachment and a host of others enable you to be in the moment and aware of the timelessness of the essential reality of creation. Non-detachment keeps you in the third dimension, limited by time and space.

BRIDGING

The challenge you face is to translate and bridge the chasm between your worldview and that of others. The span has gotten broader. You feel stretched to maximum capacity. You have never had to deal with such extremes before (though you have always had some degree of mismatch to contend with).

This will be your reality from here on out, but taken to even greater lengths.

You must learn to deal with such extremes without being crushed each time they pull at you. If you allow yourself to feel rejected and victimized, judged negatively and abused, you are buying into disempowerment. And both immediately and ultimately, disempowerment erodes your effectiveness.

JEWELS

You are accustomed to thinking in terms of having unlimited energy and time, but limited financial resources.

Think of it as the other way around. You do have unlimited financial resources; you just haven't allowed yourself to tap into them yet.

Your time and your energy are more precious, then, than money. For they give you access to your own soul and your spiritual progress. They offer you opportunities to have meaningful interactions with others.

They provide time to be alone and time to be in nature. Time to explore and discover and find joy in the unexpected. Time to treasure relationships that are gifts from multiple dimensions.

If you see time and energy as jewels rather than stones, your life will be transformed.

STAGING

You have an exacting sense of drama that is tuned to your aesthetic sensibilities more than to a rational story line. That is good because the best story lines are rarely rational as they are evolving. Only at the end when all of the pieces of scattered confetti have been swept up and glued together, shaped and molded, prodded and gilded, do you have a sense that everything followed a linear progression after all. You see the pattern that linked every moment, every vignette, every breath that it took to create the sparkling jewel that resulted.

Rationality underscores aesthetics; form follows function. Head informs heart. And vice versa.

But back to stage setting. The key here is to recognize your role as producer, director and top-billed star of your own drama. Everyone else involved has committed to staging the play as well, but you are front and center. Things come together at the appointed time, the story line unfolds, the actors live the experience as if it were real, the audience experiences it as if it were real, and everyone claps and cries and cheers at the end.

Sometimes there's even a standing ovation.

You wrote your own story. You crafted the situations and dilemmas, characters and choices. You inspired the lines of the script and provided minute details about how they should be delivered. You had a hand in the music and the set design and the costuming. Everyone is rehearsed to perfection. You have gone over details many more times than necessary. The lights in the theater are dimming. The audience is hushed. The orchestra is poised. All eyes are on the stage. This is the one and only time the drama will be performed.

No rewrites; no revisions in character or plot; no adding or cutting, expanding or simplifying.

Unless, of course, this is improvisation, which is another option for another journal entry another day.

You are at that moment just before the curtain rises. You know who you are and what you must do next. If you get a debilitating case of stage fright, we are here to whisper in your ear.

Now, the drama.

The beauty of this play is that even though you wrote it and produced it and directed it, you are experiencing it as if you knew nothing about it at all in advance. You are both a participant and an observer in your own life. You have the perspective of the audience and of the actors onstage. You can even applaud when the play is over, though you are more likely to take a bow and graciously accept the roses.

TAPESTRY

The moments link, one after the other, creating tapestries with structure and mass, soul and spirit, all of which is called "life." As your weaving takes shape, it portends a magnificent work of art.

You must believe that.

LIGHTHEARTEDNESS

Consider the term *lightheartedness*. What do the words that comprise it mean separately? Light in the heart; heart infused with light—radiating light, creating light, embodying light.

Light heals and strengthens. The heart contains and projects.

The heart is the vessel; light is what fills it.

Without light the heart is dark and heavy. When oppression overcomes enlightenment, when darkness overpowers light, the heart is black and dense. When you are lighthearted, that chakra radiates brilliant rays of gold and pale yellow.

How do you fill your heart with light?

♦ By choosing oneness over duality.

♦ By seeing yourself as spirit in the flesh.

♦ By having the courage to create a void where there once was comfortable clutter.

♦ By taking one step at a time into the path of the unknown without hesitation or fear.

EFFECTIVENESS

What you have been experiencing recently is not so much resistance to getting back to work, but a realignment of your sense of how much time and energy it takes to get your work done. Your work is being reconfigured along with everything else, so it is appropriate that the way you approach it be redefined as well.

The more you embody oneness, the more effective you will be.

Effectiveness is a function of intention—not effort. What is your intention in doing your work? When you are clear about that, the rest will flow from you.

You are redefining how you get from one place of accomplishment to another. It is not always a rational, linear trajectory. There are many surprises along the way. Help comes from unexpected sources. Inspiration arrives unbidden.

Your former calculations of the investment required to complete a task are no longer valid. Furthermore, you do not have to be perfectionistic or compulsive to achieve a level of quality that meets your standards.

Your effectiveness is tied more to your capacity to transcend duality and embody love than it is to your ability to complete massive amounts of activity.

That is no longer necessary. You do not need that reassurance anymore. Let it go.

DUALITY

Your task is to transcend duality, to live in spirit while you also live in the material world. The current magnetics surrounding the planet support duality. On the one hand, you are aware of the existence of spirit. Sometimes the presence of spirit is even palpable to you. On the other hand, you are solidly in the physical world, addressing mundane matters and paying little attention to spiritual transcendence.

To have the reality of the other side hidden from you so that you can live out your karma, to find your way to enlightenment in the middle of the darkness, everything must be designed around duality. Separateness, difference, judging and limitation all provide you with the necessary obstacles and choices that can lead you either to stagnation or transformation.

Philosophical systems such as the Tao have provided light on the path of unity with the One for millennia. But the path itself was open to only a handful of masters who could traverse it by transcending the planetary magnetics that have until now been aligned with duality.

But all of that is changing, and it is changing with lightning speed. The magnetics of the planet are being realigned to create an environment that is far more conducive to unconditional love, and that gives you far greater access to the higher dimensions.

The path is opening to all.

COMPROMISE

You have been truly joy-full lately. You are finding and fulfilling a deep part of yourself that you often do not honor adequately.

What causes you to overlook it? It is your tendency to accommodate others, which leads to your own detriment.

It is not your responsibility to be everything others want, to do everything others want, to provide everything others want, to create everything others want. It is your responsibility to do so for yourself.

When you have yourself and your spiritual development at the center of your choice process, you become more aware of the compromises you make that cost you far more than you receive in return.

Keep yourself and your soul at the center of your life. Putting others there is inappropriate and leads you to compromise—to promise against—your time and energy.

Promise for yourself instead.

ABUNDANCE

You can draw abundance to you of any sort, whether it is abundance of laughter and joy or anguish and worry.

When you choose to manifest joy is when you are balancing head and heart. When you choose to manifest worry is when you are living in imbalance, which arises from an overemphasis of either head or heart.

Your choice is always your lesson.

Notice what is currently abundant in your life. That will help you gain insight into your conscious and unconscious choices.

PARADOX

Think of your relationships in terms of a comma. Yes, a comma. A comma is made up of a point and movement. The point is steady, round, solid. The movement is fluid, curved, elastic. That is the way of love as well.

Love is like a comma—a place between two thoughts, a connection between two comments, a link between two people. But it isn't a chain link or a ball bearing link or even a ring link. It is a point for grounding, and flexibility around that point. Too much solidity or too much fluidity creates tensions in a relationship that compromise the linkage between two people.

The best relationship for you is paradoxical. You need to love with all of the power your heart can manifest. You also need to flow in and out of that love-based togetherness and into time to yourself, when you can love and nurture you alone.

Create room for togetherness and aloneness, emotion and intellect, love and friendship, passion and practicality, transcendence and the mundane, physical tenderness and spiritual union. Create room for paradox.

INTENSITY

You want very much to be in a happy, healthy relationship with a man. You also know that it does not matter at all if your life doesn't go in that direction. How can you hold both concepts in your head and your heart at once? You are already doing so to some extent. This is the point you need to reach in order to be detached enough and interested enough to achieve the appropriate outcome.

You have been both priestess and best friend to the men in your life. That was quite a package for them to accommodate. It would have been much easier for them if you were a little less complex, a little less strong-willed, a little less intelligent, a little less eccentric, a little less of a perfectionist.

It would also have been easier for you if you were.

But you're not.

Where you erred was in the intensity with which you began your relationships. Getting swept away by the initial passion and intrigue enabled both of you to sidestep sources of potential conflict and competition. And as you know all too well, the denial of those dynamics led ultimately to devastating conflict and competition.

The only way you can build a relationship with a man that has a ghost of a chance of enduring the tugs and traumas of being together is if you enter into it realistically from the beginning. That requires you to be everything that you are and to embrace everything that he is.

But not all at once!

COMMUNITY

Life is rich with opportunities to learn about yourself and others. It carries moments of poignant anticipation and regret; it creates situations that invite heartache and celebration, abandonment in love and unmitigated aloneness. It displays many facets of the same jewel—the jewel that is each person individually and in community.

You have experienced one more aspect of the global community and of yourself in that community. Being in Paris has already launched you well beyond your previous existence. You carry her gifts in your heart as well as in your luggage.

GRATITUDE

It is easy to be grateful when things are going well. At those times the heart is so full, gratitude seems to flow from an infinite source of love and joy. But the deepest gratitude arises when the heart is bereft of things to be grateful for, and in their place finds the same love and joy emerging as a result of nothing in particular.

When you are in the middle of uncertainty or fear and are able to find a pool of peace and gratitude within, you know you have tapped into gratitude of spirit rather than material gratitude.

You flow in and out of peace these days. Some moments are easier to deal with than others, but at times fear grabs you by the throat and strangles all the gratitude from your consciousness.

Fear is good at doing that. Gratitude suffocation is its specialty, along with disempowerment and cynicism.

Your lesson is to look clearly at the catalyst for the fear and with an open mind decide if there is anything you can do to address the issue—then do it. Your lesson is also to open your heart to the situation causing the fear, which arises from limited courage, and breathe it in.

Love the fear-causing moment. It is a great gift to you. The most fear-causing circumstances carry within them the most profound lessons. For they give you the opportunity to act with courage, to reaffirm your strength of heart.

LIVING in the MOMENT

Your office at home is like a little nest where you are held in light and love and music.

Here you are on a foggy Sunday morning typing away at the computer, with melodies wafting over and through you. Acknowledge all of the conditions, factors and people in your life that enable you to be doing this right now.

There is little about your life that you would change. Why? Because there is little you would rather do at this moment than manifest this message in this environment and read it when it has concluded.

This is the key to living in the moment. You have difficulty with the concept because you believe that occasions when you are doing exactly what you want are rare. That is because you do not appreciate the grace inherent in each moment.

Take the time to ask yourself, is there something I would rather be doing right now? If the answer is yes, the next question is, then why not do it? The excuses that you use to keep from doing what comes from the heart are usually insignificant. If the answer is no, then you have the opportunity to appreciate the moment—whether it involves slicing bread for toast or getting out of breath walking up a steep hill—and all of the blessings embodied within it.

So is there something you would rather be doing right now? The answer is a simple yet profound no. It echoes within your heart, making this moment as beautiful as it is complete.

FELLOWSHIP

Fellowship occurs in many ways, all of which result in communion with spirit. Fellowship is fundamental to the human condition. Those who do not experience it lash out at others because of their deep sense of spiritual rejection and what they perceive to be its root cause—their own unworthiness. They displace one form of rejection with another, rebelling against their family, friends or society. Those who do experience fellowship find it easier to weather life's inevitable vicissitudes because of the psychological safety net it provides.

Spirit is the catalyst for fellowship. Fellowship is not just about being with others, but about sharing a communion with others. Communion is community spirit—imbibing spirit together. Mutually acknowledging that consciousness surrounds and protects enables people to surround and protect each other more effectively.

Fellowship, then, is about living consciously together. It strengthens the power of spirit throughout the family and the community. You will recall that the temples of Atlantis served the purpose of bringing down spirit and blanketing the community with it. The same is true for many modern-day gatherings of people, as long as they are together in spirit.

You would be surprised to know some of these communal gathering spots. We can identify them by the energy vibration they radiate. You have been drawn to many of them; others you avoid. Some examples:

♦ Neighborhood cafes, where people share tables and newspapers, recreating the sense of family among strangers who aren't really strangers at all

♦ Movie theaters, where people experience together the deepest human emotions through drama

♦ The labyrinth at the cathedral, where people reenact their journeys under the watchful eye of spirit

♦ Subways and busses, where passengers' wordless communion is every bit as powerful as what we see emanating from many places of formal worship

♦ Clusters of urban apartment buildings, with windows that open up each neighbor's daily life to others

You are surprised at this list because it seems so anonymous and impersonal. That is the point. You and your neighbors choose to share spirit despite your never having met formally. You could put up barriers, refuse to partake in the communion, yet you choose not to.

Do not discount the spiritual power of your community of apparent strangers or your ability to create fellowship amidst the demands and detours of the day. For communion confirms spirit—your own and everyone else's—and thus extends the power of love from wherever you are out into infinity.

SAFETY NET

Your life unfolds before you like a mystery come to pass.

For more than a decade you have been moving rapidly toward the confluence of opportunity and capability, desire and readiness. The time has come for all that has been put into play to come to fruition. Like the wedding you participated in this weekend, the union of souls and situations, contribution and commitment is about to occur in your life as well.

The safety net is no longer necessary. There is no need to plan for the contingency of catching you before you fall.

Because you won't fall. You won't fall.

This is such a time in your life.

All is well.

POWER

You have been experiencing how it feels to trust—to be in your power uncompromisingly—to have the support you need to take the next steps forward. Those steps no longer feel to you like leaps of faith. Rather, your journey into the unknown seems as natural, and in many ways as easy, as one with a clear path and a map and road signs.

You have come to understand the imperative of owning your power and living from that foundational principle. We see your energy field shift every day as you integrate new dynamics of power in concert with the natural order of things.

Power that is outside the flow of nature takes on a dark character almost immediately; that is a requirement of its survival. Power that is within that flow is light—and nature—made manifest.

Never assume that acting from your power is unenlightened. Power can be used wisely or abused, and as such is neither inherently positive nor negative.

Your power derives from balancing head and heart—

from embodying your lesson. When you are in balance, there is no way you can misuse your power. When you are in balance, there is no way you can act from any other foundation but love.

For love-based power is the God-force in all its glory.

UNPREDICTABILITY

For all of your bluster and ebullience, you are still feeling insecure. So much is still unknown; so much remains to be revealed to you.

That is the natural order of things. Life flows day-to-day with the rhythms of nature. New landscapes appear; old, familiar ones remain steadfastly there for you. You cannot rush the arrival of the new ones; you should not miss the opportunity to enjoy the familiar ones.

Wanting to see what is ahead creates a situation where you neither see the future clearly nor get the most value and nourishment from the present. That, of course, is a situation to avoid, for it brings you only minimal fulfillment, pleasure and growth.

You are tempted to want more than the moment provides—to extrapolate from one event to what might be the next, creating hypothetical relationships between current and future circumstances.

You cannot access the future from the third dimension because of the rigid segmentation of time on the physical plane. Compartmentalizing time makes it difficult to recognize the patterns that link what you call past, present and future. Those linkages are more obvious to us in the higher dimensions, but still they are inherently unpredictable.

As it stands, you are not feeling quite in the flow of things. It is as if you sense that something major is about to occur. You want to get ready for it, but that is not possible. Rather than surrendering to the potentialities—whatever they may be—you cast about trying to become someone you aren't in hopes that you'll be better prepared for the unpredictable.

You are best prepared for the unpredictable when you do not prepare at all.

TRANSITIONS

You are in the middle of a profound period of transition. To help you weather the vagaries and ambiguities it introduces into your life, try to approach it this way:

♦ Remain openhearted and clearheaded, and you will be resilient when the tremors arrive in your life. Remember that you are on bedrock. The introduction of new paths and people and passageways will add to your grounding—not weaken it.

♦ Do not turn away from your power. Speak your truth—always—and refrain from wanting something or someone so much that you compromise who you are or what you believe. Such compromises put you on a path of self-abnegation rather than self-affirmation.

♦ Do not be afraid to experiment. Sometimes it is necessary to leap into the unknown. Sometimes it is more fun as well to leap into the unknown. Nothing is irrevocable. If you have learned one lesson so far, it should be that.

♦ Do not try too hard to please. You are who you are,

and that person is whole unto herself. To pretend to be someone you are not creates false expectations and weakens integrity.

♦ Remember that you are loved by many. Surround yourself with people who support and challenge you from a base of love—not insecurity.

♦ Live in gratefulness for the blessings that are showered upon you every day of the year. Acknowledge also that you are a blessing to many yourself. The gifts flow both ways already. The key patterns in your life have already been established. The changes you experience are simply enhancements of your current reality.

♦ Affirm that you deserve all that is about to come to you, for the joy that you experience is abundant beyond your most optimistic envisionings.

STILLNESS and MOVEMENT

Your exhaustion floated away with the storms that loomed over the city the past few days. You feel energized and reinvigorated—quite the opposite of what you were experiencing most recently.

Do not be concerned when those moments of near-paralysis hit you. Remember that you are at one with nature, and thus your life is an immediate reflection of what is occurring in nature. When you are renewed it is because nature has passed beyond another barrier and is flying free again.

Pay attention to how your energy patterns mirror those of nature. You will be amazed at the alignment between the two.

Use each moment, whether it brings a standstill or dynamic forward movement, as an opportunity to capitalize on the natural flow of things rather than trying to fight against it. As you know, going against the flow is futile, no matter how much you believe you are capable of succeeding by doing so.

Your life is a fascinating interplay of stillness and

movement, silence and sound, standstill and progress. All of these elements are functional—and positive—if you integrate them appropriately.

Seeking movement during times of stillness is as dysfunctional as its opposite—seeking stillness when movement is required. Do not value one over the other; rather, align who you are in the moment with the natural order of things—in the moment. That brings you to oneness with God.

Have you ever been able to go against the flow and be effective? Absolutely not. Have you been 100 percent effective when you were in flow? Absolutely. What more do you need to know?

LIGHT

Light is the medium through which spiritual entities—my colleagues and yours too, really—travel and communicate. It is the Mercury of the higher dimensions because it provides the medium that connects us all. This venue is the energy field of and around light, which is the manifestation of God. So light—the God-force—unites us, surrounds us, gives us a means to be together always.

Without it spirit is weak. In places it is almost nonexistent, although it never is obliterated completely.

You follow the path of light. Even during the strongest hurricanes of fear and doubt, you have held the flame. Because of that you see the flame in others, mirroring it naturally when you are around them, even when no words are exchanged.

So what is being asked of you? You must become a much more aggressive messenger of spirit. This requires you to give up your attachments. It challenges you to transcend fear. It demands that you embrace your power unfailingly. You must commit to your mission and balance your head and your heart. But above all, you must ride the wave of chaos as it threatens to overtake those around you.

How do you prepare for this passage?

◆ Cleanse your body of all impurities and then refrain from polluting it further. Food and drink will become more and more irrelevant as time goes on, and you will find that you have lost your taste for most things that are toxic to your physical system.

◆ Unburden your life of people, material things, expectations and attachments that do not serve you in mission and lesson. You must be ruthless in this regard. Concern about hurting others' feelings will slow your progress and deplete your reserves. This can no longer be tolerated.

◆ Find time each day to receive messages from us. We have much guidance for you. Give us every opportunity to provide you with information and support.

◆ Release all assumptions about right and wrong, good and bad, abundance and lack. The external paradigm governing the planet is shifting rapidly and is, in turn, requiring you to realign the inner paradigm you have been using for so long to define reality.

◆ Always follow the light. Those who embrace it will be evident to you. Remember how this message began: Light connects us all and provides the medium for communication and oneness. Rely on your light even more than usual now.

◆ Give thanks for this extraordinary next phase of your existence and your mission.

♦ And finally, don't take anything too seriously. Everything is about to change. And you know all too well that when things are turned upside down, they are tragic only briefly before they become quite funny. Recognize the cosmic joke in everything along with the seriousness of your work. Surround yourself with those who make you laugh, for in the end they are closer to spirit than most others.

SURVIVAL

There are many ways people choose the path of survival in a world turned upside down. Usually it is with their own self-interest in mind, or perhaps their own in conjunction with that of their family. That is, of course, a short-term and limited approach—one that can lead to the non-survival of others.

A more enlightened approach to survival is to let go of the need to survive at all. If you believe that the soul is infinite; if you believe that you are at one with the God-force always and forever; if you understand that your soul's sojourn in this current embodiment is only temporary, then you will have a longer-term perspective on the notion of survival.

In fact, the survival of all of life is assured. The quality of that life—the oneness of that life with spirit—is at issue and at stake. So the challenge is not how to secure your existence in this embodiment or the ones that follow, but how to embody spirit as completely as possible while you are on the earth plane.

Think of the 80/20 rule in terms of the choices you

make daily. You spend 80 percent of your time and energy working, talking with friends, going on errands and keeping the details of your life in relatively good order. You spend the other 20 percent relaxing—writing, reading, watching the sunset.

What if you spent only 20 percent of your time and energy on the activities that currently require 80 percent, and had the other 80 percent available to do whatever you liked? What would it be? Think about it. The answer may not be as obvious as you think.

Correct. Not much would change. If you had 80 percent of your time available to do exactly as you chose, it would not be much different from what you are currently engaged in.

When you are acting from a base of survival, you find it difficult, if not impossible, to act with spirit. You forget that your soul's existence is assured, and you certainly cannot surrender to the unknown. When you act from a base of survival, you are spending 80 percent of your effort accomplishing 20 percent of your purpose for being in embodiment (at best).

But when you act from an inner knowing of the perpetual existence of the soul, you cannot possibly spend 80 percent—or even 20 percent—of your time and effort pursuing unenlightened ends.

So the critical factor is not what you do but how you do it, and what you are assuming when you do it. Here are some questions to help with this assessment:

- When you are working, do you remain objective about the situations in which you find yourself?
- When you are having dinner with friends, do you share your spirit with them?

- When you encounter a stranger on the street or the telephone, do you treat that person with respect?
- When you declare your deepest truths and listen to another's, do you acknowledge the extraordinary privilege it is to share such intimacy?
- Do you integrate your closest relationships from the perspective of multiple lifetimes rather than just this one?

Your survival in this embodiment is relevant only to the extent that it affords you time to pursue your mission and lesson. Otherwise, it is only a third-dimensional priority, and a myopic one at that.

RESOURCEFULNESS

Think of the roots of the word *resourcefulness*. Full of resources. To re-source in a way that maintains fullness.

What are the most valuable resources on the spiritual path? What does it mean to re-source as you pursue your journey? How are you currently re-sourcing your life?

♦ You are embarking on what will be a lifelong priority of maintaining your body as a finely tuned vessel for spirit. That is a step toward re-sourcing your life.

♦ You are also rethinking how your work might best be configured, and thus are re-sourcing your financial security.

♦ You are creating new modes of accessing other dimensions through higher consciousness and awareness. This results in the re-sourcing of spirit.

♦ And finally, you are opening to love and pain equally, which re-sources the source. That is the highest of all callings.

What is fullness? Fullness requires emptiness before it can be aligned with spirit. You must clear out all the toxic thoughts, prejudices, judgments and assumptions that currently fill your mind, body and spirit. Only then can you begin to make enlightened choices about what you will allow into that emptiness to create fullness.

You know how it feels to be full of pure love and light; you also know how it feels to be full of pain and darkness. You are making choices that are moving you rapidly toward embodying the former on a more constant basis, but you still have levels and layers to probe and pursue. We ask you to persist in this. The results will astound you.

Resourcefulness that enhances and honors spirit is possible only after emptying, then re-sourcing from a place of profound awareness.

CELEBRATION

To celebrate is to honor the spirit of another in its most profound light. To celebrate is to create avenues for friends and family to come together for the purpose of ritualizing a momentous event.

To celebrate is to say to another:

♦ We love you.

♦ We are proud of you.

♦ We see your infinite beauty and character.

♦ We recognize the contribution you have made and will continue to make with your life.

♦ We will be there for you later during those forlorn times when you cannot identify anything at all about your life to be celebrated.

Celebrations raise the spiritual vibration of all participants. They are also gatherings of entities from many dimensions. We love such occasions and create quite a crowd around the celebrants.

Prepare your home to be the chapel of wisdom and joy that best serves the celebrations you host.

And don't forget to chill plenty of champagne.

CONSCIOUSNESS

Each action you take has repercussions on other planes. Every thought that skips through your mind influences the well-being of all of life. Each intention you harbor, whether it is conscious or sequestered, has an impact on the magnetic vibrations within and around you.

You see situations from the third-dimensional reality that they represent. You also accept that equally relevant realities are being played out on other dimensions, although they are not immediately evident to you.

So whenever you acknowledge that other forces beyond the physical plane are at work in every situation—yes, every single one—you are more capable of being love in the middle of whatever is occurring.

And when you are being love, you are embodying the highest consciousness.

The road to enlightened consciousness requires you to expand your awareness beyond what you see happening around you. Your immediate circumstances represent the way that larger forces are engaging in the karmic dance, be it one of wickedness or transcendence.

Look for the story behind the story, the message within the messages, the frame that redefines the immediate picture you see. Factor that into all of your perceptions. Notice when you forget to do so. That signals an area in your life where you are more deeply rooted in— and thus limited by—the myopia of the third dimension.

Notice as well when you naturally look for linkages beyond the obvious, for in those moments you are more aligned with consciousness. And more likely to be love.

TIME ALONE

You fill a great deal of your time alone with unnecessary busy-ness. When you do that you squander valuable moments and opportunities for inner growth and self-discovery. Rather than wasting that time you should be reveling in it, for it is a gift of immeasurable value and importance.

Time alone is time with spirit. When you have moments by yourself, you make room for new insights that help reframe your thinking. You let your heart beat a little more slowly and allow your life's rhythms to be a bit less staccato.

When you have time to yourself, you can recharge your energy and rejuvenate your sense of self. You do not need to accommodate others. You derive great joy from the simplest of pleasures.

Acknowledge the blessings that such occasions offer you, for soon you will have far less time to yourself than you do now. Do not wait until then to cherish your solitude.

HOPEFULNESS

These are times of tremendous upheaval, both interior and exterior. Although the catalyst for the chaos is not evident, it is present nonetheless, affecting everyone in powerful ways. These times call for hopefulness.

Hope emerges when you see the divine order of things even in the midst of disorder. It is not a naïve expression of innocence. It is not a saccharine display of positive perspective. It is not an artificial overlay of superficiality to blanket worries and concerns.

Rather, hope derives from the deepest trust that no matter how out of balance things seem, no matter how threatened your sense of security, no matter how desperate your survival demands seem to be, there remains a pool of serenity. And dipping into that pool is possible only if you are able to trust the wisdom and benevolence of the God-force, which ultimately is creating the conditions of change.

The world is no longer linear. What was a possibility one moment is not even slightly an option the next moment. What you believe to be true at noon is false by sunset. What appeared to be the right thing to do on Monday is absolutely inappropriate on Friday.

And so it goes in a world turned upside down.

You must be able to set aside all assumptions and preferences if you are to be a clear channel of spirit.

You are learning the degree to which you hang on to these viewpoints in order to maintain stability in the middle of massive change.

Refrain from creating the illusion of stability by grasping hold of outmoded beliefs and threadbare attachments. Instead, trust in and surrender to the will of God. Anything other than that is not an adequate anchor during turbulent times. It is not an appropriate anchor during any other times, either.

So we return to hope. On the one hand, you see everything changing before you. On the other hand, the most fundamental aspects of your life are changing only in that they are becoming more stable and integrated into your essence. This strengthens the core within your being and thus your hope that at the dawn, the crystal of light and love will prevail.

OBSTACLES

Why do we put obstacles in your path? If there were any way at all for us to avoid doing so, we would. But you must be tested and pushed and taken to the line over and over again, so that you will be strong enough and secure enough to undergo the transformation that is ahead for you. It will take courage that stretches far beyond your current sense of your capabilities.

The only way you can understand and accept what you are capable of is to experience it firsthand. And the only way you will ever experience your capabilities firsthand is if you encounter obstacles in your path. You would never willingly introduce them into your life, so we must do that for you.

Something is an obstacle only if you have an attachment related to it. If there is no attachment, there can be no obstacle. The most effective way to remove an obstacle is to let go of the attachment that makes it manifest. That is detachment.

And what is the quickest route to detachment?

♦ Surrender to the will of God.

- Trust that God's will is all-loving.
- Accept whatever occurs as being God's will, even if it seems to be anything but divine.

Your concerns about your long-term financial security create the biggest barrier to your enlightened progress, for they are rooted in your greatest fears and thus your greatest attachments. Your worry about growing old with inadequate financial reserves overwhelms your trust that as long as you are on mission and in lesson, abundant resources will be available to you. That is a universal law.

On some level you do know that. But third-dimensional limitations keep you attached to security-based needs.

So whenever you need to be challenged in order to reaffirm your inner strength, the most effective catalyst for that is finance-related and thus work-related.

When you no longer are so driven to secure your financial future—when you believe to and through your bones that the work and the income will be there as it always has been—the terrain of your work will look more like Illinois farmland than the San Francisco hills.

Until then, expect to encounter one hill after another. It will make you strong—perhaps unnecessarily so. And if you are also doing your inner work, it will help you shed the attachments that keep you climbing those hills.

This is difficult, demanding and exhausting work. But it also can be energizing, inspiring and creative. Try to focus as much on the latter as the former when you face the obstacles that are ahead.

COMPLETION

You have been doing a great deal to achieve balance and closure regarding many of the karmic ties that influence your relationships. This is critical work, for the release of karma by one individual also releases it for the other. It heals both people at a deep level. That healing liberates your own and others' spirits to be more completely on mission and in lesson. It also frees up energy to invest in more spirit-full endeavors.

But the karmic completion that is currently unfolding goes beyond the work you are doing as an individual soul in embodiment. It involves the liberation of the planet from its karmic past. This has been accomplished through the spiritual work of a critical mass of people. The operative term here is critical mass, for that has indeed been achieved.

Consider the karmic patterns that have accumulated over time on the planet. They have been rooted in value judgments and power struggles, killing and greed. They have focused on short-term acquisition with only perfunctory consideration of the longer-term life of the soul.

They were expressions of the veil of duality that has surrounded the planet. Now the veil is being lifted and dualistic patterns are no longer functional.

Already you are questioning this assertion. For all around you it appears that duality still firmly governs the planetary reality. But that is an illusion. On a larger scale human dynamics reflect oneness with God—not separateness from God. After all, when the soul leaves the body, it returns to oneness.

Only during the soul's interludes on earth does it move into duality, and even that is not real. It is simply a stage prop to create opportunities for enlightened—or unenlightened—choices.

We are telling you this: As of this moment the dynamics of duality have been neutralized.

Celebrate this with a heart full of recognition for yourself and others whose commitment to light and love created the opening that led to this shift. We are grateful to you in ways you cannot feel yet, but very shortly your own rapid progress will enable you to experience the God-vibration we are sending you. Until then, rest and renew.

There is still a great deal of work to be done. There is also all the support you and others need to achieve the karmic completion we envision.

SELFLESSNESS

You struggle with choices related to your commitments, both personal and professional. Reports and memos, faxes and mail (voice or electronic or on paper) overwhelm you. Given the choice, you would almost always rather be alone, or at most engage in brief conversations. That is not unhealthy.

Where do you draw the line? How can you be in the world and not have your interactions take such a great toll on you? Is it worth the cost? How can you know in advance what to commit to and what to avoid?

You must be ruthless in your efforts to eliminate everyone and everything from your life that is holding you back. What holds you back? Anything that takes away more of your energy than it replenishes.

If you have a jacket hanging in your closet that you must keep moving aside—and that you rarely wear—isn't it time to give it away? If you have been procrastinating about something, putting a great deal of energy into thinking about doing it but making no progress on it, shouldn't you decide either to complete the task or delete it from your to-do list? If being with a friend causes you frustration or anxiety or exhaustion, should you not choose to spend your time away from that person?

You fear that if you spend too much time alone, you will be ineffective in the working world. That is not the case at all. Your solitude is critical to your health and continued progress on the spiritual path. You must preserve as much time as you require—at all costs.

To be of service you need not be at the mercy of others' requests and agendas and opinions. You are at the mercy of no one's preferences but your own, and we are working with you to realign those.

Do not hesitate to make choices that support your own path. If there is any question whatsoever about whether you should do something or talk with someone or have dinner with an acquaintance, decline the invitation. Period. You cannot continue to please and appease.

So what is selflessness? It does not involve sacrificing yourself for the good of another. For in the long run, how does that help either of you? Rather, selflessness requires you to choose the path of spirit that is most closely aligned with your mission and lesson. It puts spirit, mission and lesson before your short-term self-interest. And it goes without saying that selflessness puts your spirit, mission and lesson before the interests of others.

To be selfless is to be willing to set aside the easy yes that leads eventually to the difficult no. Wouldn't you rather begin with a clear no that leads to no more difficulty?

The choice is yours.

FORTHRIGHTNESS

To be forthright is to come forth with right action.
What is right action? It consists of words and deeds that
are aligned with spirit. You are aware of many ways in
which you can achieve and maintain that alignment.

But how, exactly, can you come forth effectively?

Forthrightness is not self-righteousness, which
derives from ego—the desire to prove yourself correct
and others wrong. Ego-based motivation typically has
one agenda: exhibiting ways in which you are better than
the other. In extreme cases you act self-righteously in
order to demonstrate how you are more holy than
another. This behavior indicates the opposite about you,
of course.

So to be forthright is not to set about building a
strong case for your opinions or actions in order to con-
vince others to go along with them. It requires instead
that you simply be.

The act of simply being must be incorruptibly at one
with spirit. It breathes of a comfortableness with yourself
in your environment, even if it is inhabited mainly by

people who do not share your vision and values. Being forthright means that whatever the pervasive surrounding influence from others—whatever the direction of mass consciousness—you must stay your own course.

It is not necessary to assume the accepted worldview. Nor is it necessary to exhort people to change it, for that establishes circumstances that fuel self-righteousness. It is necessary only to act and speak in a way that recognizes and honors spirit in yourself and others.

That is the essence of forthrightness.

PERSEVERANCE

To persevere is to endure a long period of trials and tests with strength of body, mind and spirit. To endure while making body, mind or spirit vulnerable is to survive—not persevere.

You have faced many challenges in the past year. Did you persevere the bumps and bruises without eroding body, mind and spirit? The only way you can answer that question is to assess where you are now compared to where you were twelve months ago.

First, did you maintain or improve your physical stamina? Consider the condition your body was in a year ago. You were still weak from the serious illness that had put you flat on your back. Now your body is much more able to withstand the assaults of daily living. You have stopped eating and drinking many of the things that are bad for your health. You are walking long distances every day. So yes, you have persevered effectively where your body is concerned.

Mentally how well have you done? Your mind has never worked better. You are calmer and more thoughtful, whether you are devising a new corporate framework or considering a personal issue. You are far less stressed than you were a year ago. You have interludes every day when you are relaxed and at peace. Though you could expand those moments both quantitatively and qualitatively, you are making better choices that serve your mental well-being.

Spiritually you have gained access to deeper inner knowing. You have made many breakthroughs, most of which you do not yet recognize. Your spirit is whole and bright and loving. You embrace the larger reality more than you used to. You are coming home to spirit, moving at a rapid pace.

So how well have you persevered over the peaks and valleys? You have done extremely well. Recognize the soulfulness with which you have been approaching your life. Love yourself by continuing to honor your mind, body and spirit in everything you do.

ARTFULNESS

Art is an elusive word. Was Monet creating art in his garden in Giverny as well as in his renderings of the lily pond? Is art a meal you prepare to share with friends, complete with striking table settings? Can the way you approach your life, your work and your solitude be considered art?

It is possible to attain a supreme artfulness in all of these examples. For art derives from the blending of spirit and practice. Anything that is devoid of spirit cannot be artful; the greatest art is in harmony with nature and therefore carries its most profoundly simple yet sophisticated aesthetic.

So artfulness embodies spirit, nature and aesthetic harmony.

That sounds great, but how can you possibly remain artful amidst the cacophony of the day? How can you be artful in response to a driver who runs a red light or a person who sneaks in line at the post office? How can you respond artfully to someone—be it a stranger or a friend—who needs more from you than you can give?

How can you remain artful when business competitors undercut your work? Aren't there times when artfulness is impossible, if not inappropriate?

No, there are none.

Artfulness requires you to acknowledge each situation for what it is. This enables you to be fully engaged in it without judging it.

♦ Be honest and forthright without making anyone wrong. If you cannot do that, refrain from taking action or exchanging any words.

♦ Do not create a pecking order. Spirit neither recognizes nor tolerates the classification of people as "good" or "bad," "better than" or "worse than."

Artfulness arises from at-oneness with spirit. Living artfully requires you to pay attention to how you address the details of the day and the attitude with which you approach each situation. This includes encounters with yourself, for you judge yourself far more harshly than you do others. You are your own worst critic, especially during those tougher times when you could choose to give yourself encouragement rather than criticism.

Release yourself from the predisposition to judge yourself and others, and you will find that your life is indeed more artful.

And more serene.

TIMING

You will recall the line from the *Tao Te Ching*, "In action, watch the timing."

That is good advice. Niccolo Machiavelli understood that principle. So did the Japanese at Pearl Harbor.

Timing influences effectiveness as much as actions do. The right action at the wrong time can lead to the opposite effect that it would have if the timing had been better calibrated. The wrong action at the right time can squander a valuable opportunity. The right action at the right time can yield extraordinary breakthroughs.

You have an astute sense of timing. You read situations sensitively, then frame what you are seeing and feeling into multiple layers that portend different potentialities. When you have the option of calculating and calibrating the timing of something, you are rarely off the mark.

Why does this timing work so well? Because it is aligned with the flow of things that is already influencing the outcome you desire. Good timing follows the flow; bad timing swims upstream against it.

But there is another more profound way to think about timing: that the flow of things will lead you to the outcome anyway.

Think of all of the times in your life when synchronicity brought you to a particular place at a particular time so that a particular event could occur. Could you have planned all of the details that led to that outcome? Not even slightly. Could you have anticipated that a unique intersection of place and circumstance was approaching, and thus have fine-tuned your actions and timing in order to arrive there at the perfect moment?

Of course not.

Could you have spun out enough potentialities and trajectories to have predicted what was essentially unpredictable? The question answers itself.

The most astute timing transcends your capacity to maneuver and manipulate, position and project. For those actions are based on restricted access to information and thus maneuverability.

Let go of the need to control or even influence timing. Open to the patterns and prospects that you can neither recognize nor imagine. Then you access the magic —and the infinite potential—of timing as it exists beyond time.

TRANSPARENT REALITY

The observable dynamics of a situation represent one level of assessing your current reality. But many other factors that may be transparent to you—beyond your ability to recognize on the earth plane—are at work in the higher realities. In order to see the apparently transparent, you must raise your consciousness and tap into these higher dimensions. You must transcend what seems so apparent to you in the third dimension that you believe it does not warrant further consideration.

That apparent reality is only an illusion.

Let's look at a simple example.

Last week you thought you were going to the sea for some rest, but you were really there to be a catalyst for the healing of your new niece and a support to her parents after she was admitted into a hospital halfway across the country. When you heard how critical her health was, you called upon the powerful healing capabilities of your friends in that beach community. They helped your niece turn a corner in her healing process.

In this case the higher reality was transparent or

invisible to you at the time you made the decision to go for a respite at the beach. The apparent reason for your choice was simply a red herring; the actual reason was not revealed to you until later when you began working with the metaphysical and spiritual healers there to help your niece recover.

As you become more adept at tapping into higher realities, the transcendent purpose for your actions will become evident to you sooner. You will then be able to factor that purpose into your decisions more proactively—and act on it more effectively.

TRUSTWORTHINESS

To trust is to have enough confidence in yourself or another to let go of the need to control many aspects of a situation. To be worthy of trust is to commit to acting with your own or another's best spiritual interests in mind. To be trustworthy is to help yourself and others take steps to align spirit and action, words and deeds, inner and outer reality.

You must be more thoughtful when you assume that what you commit to is worthy of your trust. Is it really something you can support with all of your caring and intellect? Is there room for spirit along with everything else? Do you have the opportunity to enlighten as well as teach? Can you challenge people spiritually and mentally? If so, then the opportunity to contribute is worthy of your participation. You can commit to be trustworthy.

Trustworthiness goes both ways.

You believe that once you make a commitment you are bound by your word to honor it, even if you discover later that the larger context is anything but honorable.

That is not appropriate. Engage only in situations

that you trust are worthy of your involvement. If you do not trust the good intentions of those involved, or if they are pursuing ends unworthy of your investment of time and energy, do not agree to participate.

If later on you discover that what you thought was worthy of your trust is not worthy of it after all, then you have every right to cease your involvement in it. You need to be trustworthy only to the extent that the situation or person is worthy of your trust.

Trustworthiness is always a two-way street. If it is not, it is lacking in spirit and thus should be the work of another.

TRANSCENDENCE

To transcend is to ascend beyond the ordinary. To go far beyond normal limits. To rise above difficulty and push away obstacles. To create room for continued faith and optimism despite conditions and indications to the contrary.

You are being asked to transcend your third-dimensional reality. You are being tested to see how far you can be pushed and still transcend. You are being required to step through and far, far beyond what is immediately in front of you.

How can you continue to exist in a spiritually anemic world and keep the flame of spirit hot and bright within? We have addressed this issue many times in our messages. You know the answer on an intellectual level. It is time for you to integrate it at a cellular level.

Transcendence requires you to turn to spirit—to become spirit—as you travel through each day. You are inspired by the smallest incidents: a kind word, a thoughtful deed or a humorous remark. It takes little to rekindle your spirit. If nothing around you does that, you provide the catalyst yourself. Do not go for long without fanning the flame of spirit. If necessary, find excuses to retreat for a few moments and breathe it in.

You do not realize how often you transcend your immediate material and psychological reality. When you are exhausted from the struggle, you fall into the trap of believing that you never do and never have transcended. That is not the case at all.

The key is to transcend your own belief that you are not adept at ascending beyond the ordinary. That is holding you back more than anything else. When you stop wanting to transcend and accept that you already are going far beyond normal limits, you will in fact complete the process.

You will become transcendent.

ATTRACTION

You know that the magnetics of the planet are shifting. You have been working to realign the magnetics of your own body in order to be better suited to this new vibratory environment. What has not occurred to you until now is that these magnetics are creating a different form of attraction in relationship.

For magnetic attraction to occur, there must be polarity. On planet earth, human polarity revolves around the masculine and the feminine. The old magnetics maintained this polarity through duality. Men were totally male and women were totally female. The basis for their mutual attraction was differentness, on which duality is always based. Union occurred through the merging of opposites. The eternal question has been, will the male or female dominate?

But the planetary magnetics no longer support such duality. The basis of the new magnetics is unity and oneness. The focus has shifted from opposition to integration. Women are integrating masculine qualities into their sense of being, and men are integrating feminine qualities. Men are becoming more like women and women are becoming more like men. Both are becoming androgynous.

Polarity is still necessary for magnetic attraction, but its basis has now changed to one of complementarity. The androgynous energy patterns of the two people are so similar, their union can more naturally form a synergistic whole. This derives from reaching a significantly higher level of integration along a number of dimensions: each person's own internal alignment, the alignment of both people together, and their oneness with the God-force that is stimulated by their union. They become at one with each other and with spirit.

This transformed oneness alters the dance. The male no longer "leads." The female no longer "follows." After all, leading and following are not necessary between equals. The partners move and breathe as one.

LOVE

Love is the pure essence of God.

Love is what unites all of life with an empathetic in-tunedness. It is the vehicle that enables you to transcend the mundane considerations of life and focus on the larger reasons you are here—with others—at this moment in time. Love is the insight that helps you see beyond the immediately obvious and feel deep connections with faces from afar.

Love creates holy spaces between people—places where they can exhibit their deepest emotions and fears without repercussion. Love finds a way through the brambles and around the boulders and into new vistas. Love is at home in the heart; love is what makes any-where, anytime...home.

What stops the flow of love? Fear of rejection; feel-ings of inadequacy; focus on self-protection; desire for more, always more. All of these are evidence of your dis-tance from spirit. All of these establish dynamics that move away from love, not toward it.

One sure way to suffocate the flame of love is to

demand (or even secretly desire) that it become more than it is or something different from what it is.

Love must be given freely and unconditionally; love must be accepted without strings or implications. Love must be allowed to be. Nothing more, nothing less.

Love just is, and it remains absolute when nothing more is expected of it. It is also at its most powerful when you give and receive it with no other intention in mind. The minute you express it in a way that is calculated to lead to a desired result, it loses its potency. The desired outcome actually becomes more elusive than it would have been otherwise.

Ultimately you must understand only this: Love is its own reward. All other consequences of love are moot.

So focus on the simple melodies of your innermost heart songs. They need no accompaniment.

Gates McKibbin never imagined that after spending twenty years as a corporate executive, management consultant and adjunct college professor specializing in strategic and organizational renewal, she would publish messages channeled from her deceased father, John McKibbin. For most of her adult life she had balanced a fulfilling professional career and a fascinating spiritual quest. Then quite unexpectedly her father, who visited the earth plane frequently after his death, began sending telepathic messages for her to write in her journal.

Three years and six books later, Gates has now added "Inspirational author and speaker" to her resume. She still helps business executives navigate turbulent change, and she also seeds the planet with insights from the spirit world. To complement the LifeLines Library, Gates has developed a collection of thematic LifeLines note pads featuring her favorite one-liners from the books.

Born and raised in central Illinois, Gates now resides in San Francisco. Whenever she has a few hours of free time, she hunts for vintage jackets, walks to North Beach restaurants for risotto, creates bead-bedecked greeting cards and, of course, continues her journal writing. Gates holds a Ph.D. from the University of Illinois and has received numerous academic awards, among them Phi Beta Kappa.

LIFELINES LIBRARY ORDER FORM

FEATURING BOOKS BY GATES McKIBBIN

Book Title	Quantity	Total Cost
The Light in the Living Room: Dad's Messages from the Other Side $9.95		
LoveLines: Notes on Loving and Being Loved $9.95		
A Course in Courage: Disarming the Darkness with Strength of Heart $9.95		
A Handbook on Hope: Fusing Optimism and Action $9.95		
The Life of the Soul: The Path of Spirit in Your Lifetimes $9.95		
Available Wisdom: Insights from Beyond the Third Dimension $9.95		
Complete set of six books in the LifeLines Library $39.95		
Subtotal		
CA residents add 7.35% sales tax		
Postage and handling (F.O.B.)		
Total		

Payment Information

Charge to: VISA ☐   MasterCard ☐

Card number _____ Exp. date_____

Ship to:

Name_____

Street_____ Apt._____

City_____ State_____ Zip_____

Phone: _____ Fax_____

E-mail: _____

To order by phone call (707) 433-9771

Fax your order to (707) 433-9772

Order via e-mail at **www.fieldflowers.com**

Visit our Website at **www.lifelineslibrary.com**

LIFELINES NOTE PADS ORDER FORM

Note Pads 12 messages in each pad, 108 pages	Quantity	Total Cost @ $7.95/pad
Authenticity (#LL1000)		
Boundaries (#LL1001)		
Change (#LL1002)		
Commitment (#LL1003)		
Companionship (#LL1004)		
Courage (#LL1005)		
Effectiveness (#LL1006)		
Hope (#LL1007)		
Love (#LL1008)		
Real Work (#LL1009)		
Strength (#LL1010)		
Time (#LL1011)		
Unconditional Love (#LL1012)		
Vitality (#LL1013)		
Wisdom (#LL1014)		
Subtotal		
CA residents add 7.35% sales tax		
Postage and handling (F.O.B.)		
Total		

Payment Information

Charge to: VISA ☐   MasterCard ☐

Card number _____ Exp. date_____

Ship to:

Name_____

Street_____ Apt._____

City_____ State_____ Zip_____

Phone: _____ Fax_____

E-mail: _____

To order by phone call (707) 433-9771

Fax your order to (707) 433-9772

Order via e-mail at www.fieldflowers.com

Visit our Website at www.lifelineslibrary.com